Duifie

Duifie

YOUR OWN HOME

Splendid ideas for settling in

David & Vicky Bell

Photography by Anton de Beer

δελος

Acknowledgements

The writing of this book has been a very interesting and exciting experience largely due to the generous involvement of so many people. It has been a team effort all the way, the enthusiasm and helpfulness, not to mention the hard work of everyone involved, playing a large part in the success of this book.

We have been extremely fortunate to have been allowed into many innovative homes. The generous spirit in which we were given access to precious collections and so many new ideas is much appreciated. We would like to extend our thanks to good-hearted hosts Peter and Gill Atterbury, Philien and Craig Webster, Kitty and Steve Cruise, Mike and Sue Dall, Richard King, Richard Perfect and Tony Robinson, George and Kirsty Tatham, Louise and Adriaan Vorster, Nikki Smuts and Drummond Mello.

Very special thanks must go to Anne Balfour-Cunningham, who not only allowed us to photograph her home but also helped tremendously in styling many of the pictures.

Peter Atterbury and his patient wife deserve special thanks for the many hours he spent on the layout and planning of the book.

To Anton de Beer, our valiant photographer, who made himself available at all sorts of irregular hours and was tirelessly enthusiastic, goes great praise.

Philien Webster, another team member, needs special thanks for the beautiful illustrations.

Finally, Giovanna Martini, who under great pressure typed the manuscript — many thanks.

© 1991 Delos Publishers, 40 Heerengracht, Cape Town

Photography by Anton de Beer
Illustrations by Philien Webster
Book design by Peter Atterbury
Cover design by Etienne van Duyker

Set in Bodoni 11 on 13 pt.
Printed and bound by Toppan Printing Company (H.K.),
Hong Kong
First Edition 1991

ISBN 1 86826 136 0

CONTENTS

Foreword	6
Introduction	7
Starting Points	9
Back to Basics — The fundamental framework of the home	17
Sitting Pretty — Living and eating rooms	29
What's Cooking — Kitchens	49
Under the Covers — Bedrooms	61
Water Works — Bathrooms	71
Conclusion	80

Foreword

This book is aimed at all who feel that they need a fresh start in decorating their homes and particularly first-time homemakers. It is intended as an ideas book, an encouragement to open yourself up to what is available in order to identify what will work for you. As far as possible, we do not attempt to prescribe to any particular decorating style, although, obviously, our own style and taste will come through. We acknowledge the importance of your uniqueness and the need to create an environment reflecting your own style and personality.

We try to steer you away from unquestioningly following prescribed traditional and expected norms in favour of making a new set of your own.

This approach demands confidence, which is why it is important to determine a starting point to explore and establish your own taste. Thorough consideration, combined with confidence, is vital if you are to create convincing results.

Give yourself plenty of time to think about what you are doing. It is necessary to feel inspired, but don't allow your enthusiasm to get in the way of a satisfactory end product. Decorating your home should be something that you never complete and it should never be static. It should be an ongoing process, evolving and developing as you, the occupants of the space, mature and change.

We are certain that there is great satisfaction and fulfilment to be derived from the appreciation and refinement of your own sense of colour and style.

Introduction

Decorating your own home for the first time or revamping an existing one can be a tremendously exciting challenge. It can also seem to be a monumental undertaking. There are so many possibilities and endless choices and most of them seem so expensive. Most important is to establish what you really like, what would suit your room and your life style and your general direction. Once this is done, you are on your way.

The ideas that have given this book its form stem from several fundamental needs. They can be summed up in four words – honesty, quality, cost and practicality.

First, and foremost, is the need to create a home environment that honestly reflects the personalities of the people living in it. It is important to have established what it is that appeals to you in terms of interior decoration. Many people are reluctant to be original or creative in any way when it comes to decorating their homes. Be bold. Personal style demands confidence. If every item in your home is one that you really and honestly like, the end product will say a great deal about you.

Second, choose quality above quantity. This will generally tie in with cost. You will obviously need to work within the framework of a comfortable budget and you need to plan accordingly. Nonetheless, even on a small budget, we recommend that you start with a few quality basics and slowly build on them. Try not to compromise. Spend the largest part of your budget on the things that you are going to use most and that you want to last for a long time. As in your clothing wardrobe, a few good quality basics that you really like go a long way combined with a few inexpensive accessories. Likewise, good quality basic furniture and fittings provide the basis onto which you can impose personality, fashion and exciting detail with things that are easily changed like curtains, pictures, wall colours, rugs or even a huge bowl of flowers. A living room furnished with only two beautiful chairs and an indoor tree will be much more dramatic than a room full of compromises. It is really not worth being shortsighted or impatient.

Lastly, there is no point in having a beautiful home that is not comfortable and practical. You need to consider the practicality of every item that you put into your home and, most particularly, of the things that will be used regularly. Your life style will also play a major role in your choices – think about whether the objects you choose will fit in with the way you would like your family to live and the space available. Unless you are warm and comfortable and the furnishings and fittings serve their purpose well, you cannot relax and enjoy your home.

If you take all these aspects into account when decorating your home the end result can only be successful and exciting.

Starting Points

People often feel that, if they don't know exactly what they want in their homes from the start, thet don't have any style. Everybody has a unique style — sometimes it is just not very clear cut or the person is too self-concious to express it. In any event, any really individual home has to evolve slowly. This is often more than half the fun of making your own home.

The biggest dilemma facing the new homemaker is how and where to start.

For each person the starting point can be a totally different source of inspiration. You may, for example, already have some good pieces of furniture, some beautiful pieces of crockery or even a stunning carpet or two. Consider carefully what you have that you particularly like. Define loosely what it is that appeals to you about the object. Is it the shape, the colours, the design, the finish? Once you have isolated what it is, explore further. Build up a collection of fabric swatches, objects, cups and saucers and anything that carries this theme through. Collect plenty of magazines and page through them. When you see a picture of an interior that you really like, tear it out or mark it. Once you have a pile of these, go through them and identify what common elements are amongst them. Perhaps the colouring is the same. Perhaps it is a particular style that you identify with. Isolate these elements and think about how they would suit your home. Never think in terms of duplicating the exact scene in your home. An illustration is meant to be merely a source of ideas. It is you who must put them to work in your own rooms. It is your combinations and adaptations that will determine your own personal style.

As far as colour schemes are concerned, a whole host of sources can provide you with the inspiration you need. Cups and plates, even old rugs and hand-knitted multy coloured jerseys can be just the spark you need. They can prove to be a rich source of reference material, wonderful examples of colour combinations that harmonise or contrast successfully. Look at postcards, wrapping paper and anything else that stimulates the visual senses. It helps to keep a file of all these ideas, especially if you are going to take quite a while to complete your decoration. It will serve as a constant source of reference and motivation – even perhaps once you have finished your redecoration.

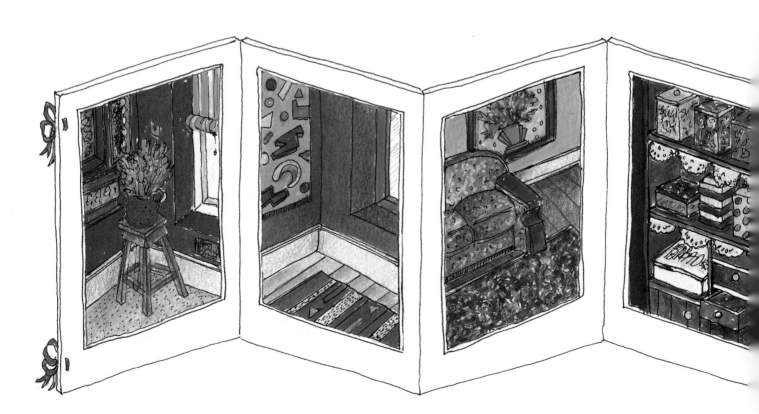

Travel is a very exciting way of broadening the scope of your ideas and your sense of style. The way other cultures decorate their buildings can be unusual and exciting. The bright, crisp simplicity of the white modern Greek homes contrasted with their sky-blue window frames and shutters or maybe even the grandiose treatment of a splendid old European hotel can set your mind going. One is not always conscious of inspiration — one often absorbs influences without being aware of it. Foreign travel can make you more attentive and open to new ideas, as you are removed from everything familiar and expected.

Traditionally, interior decoration is treated in the media in a way that makes it difficult for one to imagine that this is what your house can look like. Don't be discouraged by magnificent or exotic pictures or terribly expensive furniture. Even if you intend to decorate your home on a shoestring, you can still create a very exciting end result.

Mix-and-match co-ordinates that are extensively marketed and very practical also pose a problem. They mostly work as co-ordinates only within a particular concept. Change a colour or introduce furnishings or fabric of your own choice and you are very often faced with a jarring combination. This mix-and-match concept, although simplifying home decoration, also tends to stop you exploring other options.

If your home is to be decorated with honesty and individuality, it is up to you to develop it and to choose things because you really like them and not because you think you are expected to like them. Whenever you buy anything for your home be very conscious of the decorative as well as the practical elements of the item. Ideally it should not only serve its purpose but it should also have a design that you find attractive. This approach requires quite a bit of patience, as you need plenty of time to build up a good col-

lection. It can be frustrating but is can also bring great satisfaction. It is certainly not the same as making your selection from a glossy brochure and having your chosen items delivered and installed the next week. Everyone is inclined to be impatient but it is important not to drop your standards or make any compromises. Buy your basics first. Try to stay with good quality even if it means having or doing less and stick to your ideas once you have researched and decided upon them. As a room takes shape, your ideas will certainly develop. Stay on track, see it through. Remember, if the end result is going to be good, it is worth waiting for.

Collections

A collection of objects disco-vered and loved individually can be one of the most effective starting points. What people collect can often prove to be an integral part of who they are. We have been collectors for as long as we can remember; not always of the same things but one collection we have found, often grows from another. Some of the objects have proved valuable financially and others valuable only to us, but all of them we have found beautiful or interesting and they are generally cherished possessions. What we have collected affects the direction we take in decorating most of the rooms in our home. You will obviously have your own ideas of what is attractive or what you'd like to collect. A collection need not be made up of what is traditionally collected, although such items are usually particu-larly appealing if they have a clear theme, style or di-rection.

A collection is a group of objects chosen because of a common ele-ment that unites them. It provides you with a good excuse to buy a variety of things that you love. They need not be objects that are expensive, although of course many collections are. The greatest satisfaction of a collection is to build it up slowly adding one object at a time. Most collections are for display purposes and add interest and detail to a room. They can be a mood-crea-tor, a colour inspiration for a room or a means of developing the theme of a room. The element that unifies them should be as much of a contrast as a

similarity. The contrast could be in terms of colour, shape, decoration or texture. The collection need not be for display purposes only. It could just as well be your crockery or your lounge or dining-room furniture. Your dinner service could easily be a collection of plates and dishes that are all black and white but have many different patterns and styles. Not only will this save you money – it will certainly also look in-teresting and more than likely be very impressive.

As far as lounge or dining-room furniture is concerned there will need to be some unifying element that sets it apart from a haphazard group of chairs. This gives your home an exci-ting and dynamic feel and will most certainly not result in a mundane, predictable and co-ordinated look. The ad-vantage of a collection of this nature is that you can build it up slowly and you can maintain your standard of quality by buying only things that you love, when you can afford them.

Collectables have their fashions and trends too and, if you are an astute shopper and know what you are looking for, you can pick up good pieces for reasonable prices. Most towns have their junk shops and fêtes. These are very often the best places to pick up bargains if you know what you are looking for. It is best to shop with a specific direction in mind and it is also important to know when to stop.

Back to Basics

Our primary concern in this book is the interior of a home. However, we cannot ignore the exterior of a house or deny it at least some of the attention it deserves. We intend only to touch on this area here in the context of the rest of the house, as we lack the space to deal with it in any great depth.

Before you attempt the interior of your house, have a long, hard look at the exterior. The facade of your house is the first impression a person has of it so it deserves special attention. It sets the tone and character of the rest of the house. The positioning of the door, windows and chimney, the shape of the roof line, the finish of the walls, the small architectural details and, of course, the colour scheme will all affect the way a house is perceived. Often, otherwise attractive houses have been ruined by having the original architectural features thoughtlessly remodelled and character details removed. A relatively small amount of carefully considered good work on the facade can do wonders to transform your home and increase its market value dramatically.

The floor tiling is extented in an innovative way to make a dramatic feature of the entrance to this home.

Although the tiles are laid in a different pattern, the similarity in colours links the stoep to the entrance steps.

Carefully chosen pots can complement the style of the exterior very effectively.

When you renovate a house, particularly an old house, it is important to keep in tune with the style and mood of the house and the general character of the neighbourhood. The charm of a row of cottages has a great deal to do with the similarity of style and detail. If your house is semi-detached or otherwise very similar to the others in your road, rather avoid breaking away to something totally different, unless, of course, the others are run down or un-attractive. This obviously does not apply if your house and those of the neighbours are behind high walls and hedges. Small details, particularly in the case of an old house, make a considerable difference to the facade. Find out what detail was originally part of your house by looking at other houses in your area and by looking in historical books. To find replacements for lost details you may have to go to demolition yards although reproductions are also often available. Any of the original ornamentation should obviously be kept. It is very often these details that can transform the look of your house and are well worth the effort involved.

There is no denying that colour is the simplest and most dramatic way of changing the exterior of your house. Things to consider before you paint are:

- the age and character of the house,
- the environment in which the house is set and
- the quality of the light.

Bright colours work well where there is strong sunshine (think of Greece or the Natal Coast) but they do no not work as well on a lush dairy farm in the Midlands.

While a coat of paint can transform a building most successfully, it can just as easily ruin it. Before committing yourself to a colour scheme spend plenty of time outside visualising how the colours work with the colours of the vegetation that surrounds your house and the colour of the tiles or roof treatment. As far as possible never paint over stone walls. Rather brighten up the building by concentrating on the windows, doors and wooden or cast-iron detail.

The wide stoep is particularly well suited to the South African climate as an outdoor extension of the living space.

Historically correct detailing on this house enhances its aesthetic value.

This grand yet simple doorway is an imposing feature.

This classic cottage door not only allows in plenty of sunlight but also links the interior with the attractive garden outside.

The bright colours of a lemon tree directly outside bring the garden into the kitchen.

These lovely old oregon pine doors were discovered in a demolition yard and build in here, forming a cheerful entrance to a bedroom.

Windows

The most common mistake when it comes to windows is to replace original wooden windows with modern metal or aluminium ones. If you have to replace windows try to do so with ones that are similar, rather than tamper with the proportion and balance of the original facade. If you need to add windows due to extensions or lack of light, consider introducing similar windows on the back and side of the house. You should try to avoid an unbalanced, higgledy-piggledy look in any style. New windows should look as though they are part of the original building. Try to match the size of window panes and make sure that the sills and tops of windows are lined up. If windows are different in size, match up the tops.

Windows have a dramatic effect, not only on the exterior of a house but also on the interior. The difference between a dark, gloomy room and a bright, sunny one speaks for itself. A new window can make all the difference between a room that is pleasant to spend time in and one that is not. The amount of natural light in a room affects both the colours of the furnishing and its atmosphere.

The carefully selected curtaining complements the stone walls outside, highlighting the need to consider the view from the outside as much as the other features of a window.

Appropriate piantwork emphasises the traditional South African element of this home.

An original and well-considered Mediterranean approach to colour works most successfully here in a South African seaside home.

Doors

The front door is the focal point of your facade. Its treatment determines a large part of the character of your home. Pay close attention to all the details of the door — hinges, handles, knockers, porches, pediments and columns. Unless the door is made of very tough water-resistant wood or you have a broad covered stoep, it is best to paint it. You can play around with colour here to create some very interesting effects. The door and window-frames can be painted the same colour with the door painted a contrasting colour, to accentuate the detail. The colour of the door must work well with the rest of the colour scheme for the exterior.

If you have an interesting front door that is in need of repair, it is probably worth your while repairing it; it will not necessarily cost more than replacing it. It is of course possible to find beautiful old doors at very reasonable prices in junk shops and demolition yards. If your front door is unexceptional in every way and your facade is quite plain, an alternative to a little paint would be to try and find a new, exciting door that suits your house.

The practical and decorative aspects are combined here most successfully.

Interiors

At this stage we are assuming that you have done your research, that you have completed your file full of ideas and that you have at least established your starting point. Do not be over-hasty. This is the most important stage in the process of decorating your home. Think everything through thoroughly before you start shopping for anything; have a clear idea of what it is you want. Although you should stick to your basic ideas, once you have decided upon them, there should still be a bit of room for flexibility. Nonetheless, don't allow yourself to be pressurised by forceful salespeople. Do not compromise by settling for lower quality, unless your are certain that there is no other way of achieving the look you want. The kitchen is a perfect example. If you cannot afford anything but the cheapest of fitted chipboard units, consider other options. Brightly painted, inexpensive pine units, other free-standing cupboards or well thought-out shelves can be a very attractive and equally effective alternatives.

Picture the rooms you intend to decorate. Identify the positive aspects that should be accentuated. Imagine your furniture, pictures and rugs in the room. Establish the room's purpose. Think about the traffic flow through it, the storage facilities and the lighting. Experiment with colour. If you plan to lay carpets, bring home the biggest piece of carpeting sample that you can. Paint a section of the wall with the colours that you are thinking about and see what they look like in both natural and artificial light. The other elements that affect colour, like the size of the room and the finish of the walls, should also become evident.

Always try to make the best of what you have. There are so many different ways of changing and adapting pieces of furniture, amongst these being fancy paintwork, re-upholstery and bleaching of the woodwork. Before you discard anything, make sure whether or not you can transform it into something that will fit in with your plans for your home. Of course, there are limits — if you simply don't like it, especially if it is a valuable piece, it would be better to sell it and buy something else that you prefer. Very few people are in the position to furnish a house from scratch without having to contend with old pieces of furniture or curtaining that they don't feel they can throw away. Work around these, especially those pieces that you do happen to love. Have a close look at each item. If your carpet is tatty but otherwise attractive, scatter rugs over it. If that is not a satisfactory solution, see what is underneath the carpets. If there are wooden floors, strip and polish them. If the wood is in a very bad state and seems unsalvageable, paint or stencil the floor.

Make a list of changes and furnishings you will need in the room to make it as you want it to be. Then rethink it in terms of your priorities.

It is very important to be realistic about what you can afford to achieve. A budget is vital. Get detailed estimates from all the experts you are likely to need and find out the costs of all the materials. Add about 10% on to the estimated total for unexpected costs, which there will always be. Decide what you are going to do immediately. Before your tackle any job, ask yourself first if it's necessary, if you can do it properly or if it would be cheaper in the long run to employ a professional to do it for you.

The best place to start is with the basics. Do these as well and as thoroughly as you can possibly afford. Don't skimp unnecessarily on quality here. If you can get these right, you are more than halfway there. A plain room with a high-quality carpet or finely sanded floors, well-painted walls, well thought out doors and details — door knobs, splash-plates, surrounds, etc. — or a handsome light fitting is already elegant, even with only a few chosen pieces of furniture. On the other hand a room full of beautifully co-ordinated pieces of furniture can still look unconvincing if the floor treatment is shoddy, the wall finish is unsatisfactory or the light fitting is awkward or inappropriate. You need to work with the character of each room and not against it. Try to sustain the atmosphere of a home at all times. A Newlands village cottage cannot hope to work successfully with the cosmopolitan interior of a Clifton beach penthouse. One of the secrets of successful interior design is to keep everything in proportion and to use appropriate, sympathetic materials and textures. As difficult as it may seem, it is often better to live in your home before you make any major changes. You should then have a better understanding of the feel of the space, the traffic flow through the rooms, the bright, sunny areas and many other qualities peculiar to the house.

Take note of the detailing of your house. Try to keep the look of your house authentic by paying special attention to detail. Many styles, however, do work well together and one needn't be fastidiously exact. An Art Deco fireplace, for example, would not fit in a Victorian stone cottage but could work very well in a modern home. When replacing detail such as fireplaces, keep proportion in mind, as well as appropriate style. The fireplace very often acts as the focal point of your living area, the same way that the front door does for the facade. It serves as a very effective display area

and it makes sense for it to complement the room as attractively as possible.

Floors

It is very important to get the floor treatment to look right in every room. The floor forms the basis of your room and the way it is treated will have a strong influence on the general appearance and character of the room. Like everything else in the home, if you want it to look its best, you need to give it a lot of thought. There are many things to consider when choosing specific flooring. First and foremost you must bear in mind the function of the room — is it for washing or sleeping in? Is it perhaps to be a heavy traffic area or a room that is seldom used? Then there are technical issues — is the subfloor sufficient to cope with the weight of your chosen floor? How viable would it be to lay the floor and what work would be involved?

You also need to think about whether you want the flooring to enhance the architectural style of your home or the style of the furnishings. Areas that have a heavy traffic flow must be covered by a durable material and preferably not by lightly coloured carpeting. Hard-wearing fibres, like coir matting and wool, would work well in these areas but tiles and wooden flooring would obviously work best.

If the room is gloomy or south-facing you should use light colours and avoid big prints. The same applies to a small room, where you should also avoid borders, which will break up the space and accentuate the smallness of the room. Always try to have either the same colour carpet or flooring as the walls or the same colour curtains as the walls to avoid the room looking fragmented and small.

Some floor treatments suit some styles better than others. For example, a terracotta-tiled floor would complement cane furniture and scatter rugs more convincingly than a plush-pile carpet would. A very effective way of setting the tone of a period house is to use the flooring typical of the era. Although most flooring is designed to be fairly neutral for obvious reasons, certain types of flooring can serve as the basis or starting point for the decoration of a whole room. Paint techniques can be used to make a feature of a floor. This is a very decorative and interesting way of dealing with a floor. We will not even begin to elaborate on this area, as there are so many possibilities widely covered in the bookstores and libraries.

Because of the enormous variety of carpets available in colours, pile, make-up and pattern, you should be able to find something suitable for almost every room. Carpets have a quality that no other floor surface can provide. Not only are they soft to walk on, they can also create a luxurious and comfortable setting for your furniture, as well as being sound-absorbent. Neutral carpets can successfully

A variety of floor treatments:
a) imposing marble
b) hard-wearing coir
c) an exquisitely coloured rug
d) tipped oregon pine
e) parthy quarry tiles

hold together an otherwise haphazard collection of rugs that you can buy as you discover them. Rugs introduce a richness of colour and pattern and an element of interest to your room and they, too, can be a starting point for the rest of the decoration of your room.

Walls

The way you finish the walls of your rooms will make a difference to their look, mood and atmosphere. Your choices of wall treatments are almost endless, including fancy paintwork, tiling and wallpapering. There are also other suitable fabrics and finishes that you can apply to your walls, such as felt and cotton. The walls can be seen as a neutral background, an attractively co-ordinated surface or a work of art in themselves. There are plenty of books on the subject of paint techniques – suffice it to say that it is possible to create a wide range of stunning and interesting effects on your walls. Make sure that if you do

plan to experiment with paint techniques, the end result complements the style and mood of your room. Paint techniques are particularly successful in infecting interest into characterless rooms.

The colour of the walls can very easily dominate a room and it is best to consider it very carefully to ensure that the resulting effect isn't disastrous. Try out as many tones of the colour as you can. If you can't find the exact shade you want you can always have it mixed for you at a paint shop. Experiment. Remember that very often colours look lighter on the swatch and on a small area than over a whole wall. What may look like a faint touch of rose on the swatch may turn out to be a bright pink. Use dark colours with great care, as they can easily make a room seem much smaller and very gloomy.

A very light paint, especially with the slightest hint of yellow, will brighten up the smallest of rooms. It will also combine easily with many other colours in furnishings and pictures. If your home has interesting architectural features, like moulded ceilings, cornices or panelling, clever paint-

Instead of housing tatty old kitchenware, the tops of these kitchen cupboards have been used most successfully as an aesthetic feature.

work can emphasise and enhance these features, putting them to their best advantage. Not only is there a variety of effects that can be achieved with different techniques; there is also a wide choice of paint types that each produces a slightly different end result. And eggshell paint will produce a much more subtle and refined finish than an oil-based gloss. The gloss finish is best suited to metal, doors and other woodwork and has the advantage of being easy to clean. The most commonly used wall paint is a water-based emulsion.

Finally, wallpaper is another potentialy exciting solution. The quality of wallpaper depends on how washable it is and on its weight; the heavier the wallpaper, the better the quality. Some very expensive wallpaper is hand-printed. If you are choosing strongly pattened paper, think long and hard about it before you commit yourself. Try not to choose wallpaper that will lock you into a specific combination of patterns and colours.

Storage

It is often said that a large part of style is order. Bearing this in mind, storage can make a great deal of difference to the appearance of your home and the quality of your life. Everyone has possessions that need storing. Well-

designed storage systems prevent clutter and mess and the frustration that accompany it.

Your particular collection of possessions, being specific to you, obviously needs its own type of storage. Plan carefully what storage you would need and where it would need to be. Then consider the storage systems available.

- Built-in cupboards are ideal for awkward spaces.
- Modular systems can be added to as the demand increases.
- Free-standing units − if you have the space − a very wide range is available.

It is best to have an overall plan for a room and to avoid making piecemeal arrangements. Make sure that every room has the storage it requires.

Once you have completed the basic shell of your house it will look so good that you will most probably want to rush out and buy everything else you need to funish the rooms. Try to restrain youself if you can't afford it. Rather buy one very good piece at a time that will in itself be a furniture basic. Within a high quality and attractive framework each piece will look its best. Enjoy each purchase one at a time and try to purchase only pieces that you are happy to live with for the rest of your life. In this way you will build up an interior that is well considered, serves its purpose exactly and is truly representative of your style and personality.

An antique storage unit is a beautiful and thoroughly practical feature of this kitchen.

Sitting Pretty

The living rooms of your home are just that — the rooms where you will spend a great deal of your waking and active hours, where you will entertain friends, do handwork or homework and, most of all, relax. As is the case with any room in the home, the functions and purpose of the living rooms must dictate to a large extent everything about them. The space must be comfortable, warm and attractive, as well as having atmosphere in order for you and others to enjoy being in it. It must work well in terms of flow, lighting, storage and ventilation. Only if all these needs are met will it function really successfully.

A well-dressed fireplace makes a commanding focal point of this room.

Here an alternative focal point is made of a well-considered arrangement of objects.

Living Rooms

Being the living rooms, they also tend to say a great deal about the people who live in them, not only as far as how they live but also in terms of their style, personality and taste. Therefore, do not underplay the decorative aspects of the space. Nothing can be more depressing than a room that is dull, respectable and predictable, with no excitement or character of its own. The living rooms are perfect places to be daring and bold, to experiment with colour, texture and styles. There are few mandatory fittings other than seating, flat surfaces, lighting and storage and these are available in an endless variety of choices. As long as your seating is really comfortable, there is nothing that dictates what it should look like except your own style. Your home can carry off any decor you choose as long as it is well considered and you develop it and carry it through with conviction. Give the decoration plenty of thought but don't be tentative about what you are doing. This can often

lead to the dreaded dull and predictable end result. Don't ever feel that you have to follow a perfectly co-ordinated colour scheme and that you cannot mix one print with another. A colour scheme can certainly be a good guideline and a great help but don't feel that you are locked into it unless you want to be. There are no rules in colour combinations that cannot be broken if you do it with conviction.

As far as possible, your home should be planned around the people who live in it and use it. If you are fortunate enough to have two or more living rooms, you will of course, to a certain extent, be able to choose what activities happen where. Many of us, however, have only the one main living space and therefore the decoration and furnishing of the room will be dictated by the number and ages of the people who will use it. It is purely a waste of time to try and create a formal, immaculate lounge of your one and only living space if you have a couple of active

Daring use of colour makes a confident statement in this room.

young children. Rather avoid the frustrations and heart-break and bear the children in mind from the start.

This does not mean that you need to strip the room down to its bare essentials and leave it devoid of any decoration. It may just mean raising your displays and collections a few feet or putting them behind locked glass doors. Visual interest can be developed through imaginative use of colour, texture and patterns.

If you have a very busy social life and a lot of it takes place in your home, there would also be important aspects to consider to make life easier. Amongst them would be seating, durable flooring (i.e. no cream carpets, unless you have lots of rugs to scatter over them), ease of traffic flow and sufficient side tables.

It is possibly best to approach the decoration of the living areas in three stages of priority. First and foremost would be the basics, which we have already covered at length in an earlier chapter (see Back to Basics). Remember, an interesting floor treatment and richly coloured walls can immediately make a room appear warmer and more furnished. Windows justify special attention in the living

This colourful exciting collection is displayed with confidence and as a result is very effective in injecting humour and energy into the room.

room. Try to ensure that there is as much natural light as possible. It is even better to have doors opening out into the garden so that the living area can be extended outdoors in good weather. It is unsatisfactory to always have to use artificial lighting when there is daylight ouside. A sunny spot indoors to sit in in winter is a warm and wonderful bonus. Number two on the list would be the furniture and here you would start with the basics too. Quality, comfortable seating, storage and lighting are the most important elements at this stage. Buy them to last. They are the things that will be used most, so make sure that they are made of good materials and will wear well.

It helps to have a starting point for the room, perhaps a feature around which to plan the whole room. It might set the tone or dictate a colour scheme. Maybe you have a beloved and beautiful heirloom or a lovely rug of interesting colours. Develop the room slowly as you find the appropriate furnishings that you really like. Do not feel the need to rush into buying things. Any truly individual room has to evolve slowly. When it comes to couches, chairs and other furniture that is to be used constantly and that you will be

keeping for many years, don't compromise if you can possibly help it. Rather have two comfortable chairs in your living room until you can afford more than spend the money on five unsatisfactory ones of lesser quality. Second best is not good enough. Buy the best seating you can. Good design and quality are not necessarily more expensive. Very often you can buy excellent pieces of furniture second-hand at auctions or from junk shops for very reasonable prices. They may need to be re-upholstered or draped with fabric or a rug but they are generally better in terms of comfort and style than the new funiture that you could buy at the same price. You are much more likely to create a convincing effect with quality furniture and carefully selected inexpensive curtaining and accessories than with poor-quality furniture and even the most expensive curtaining and accessories.

A very important aspect of seating is its arrangement. It is generally preferable to group your seating rather than to have a random scattering. Most living rooms work best if it is possible for the seating to form a circle, square or rectangle of sorts. The seating should preferably be fairly flexible

to allow the circle to be extended for extra seats. This facilitates communication and allows for a much more relaxed atmosphere. Three-seater couches are much less suitable than two-seaters: not only do they take up more space, it is also difficult to relax sitting three in a row. Seats should also be close enough for people to talk comfortably but not too close for comfort.

The positioning of the furniture is sometimes dominated by the structure of the room. The room will normally have at least one or two obvious focal points that people are drawn to – perhaps a fire place or a view from the window. Although it is best to be able to watch television comfortably seated, it is preferable to avoid letting the television set dominate the room. It can be problematic if you have a striking fireplace and large windows with a magnificent view on the opposite wall. A way to counterbalance this would be to place a large mirror above the fireplace or at right angles to the view to reflect it back into the room.

If the room is to be used often by a lot of people, especially by children, storage becomes an important way of introducing order into the room and reducing unnecessary clutter. Storage takes up visual space and is often a strong feature of the room, so it should be carefully considered as an integral part of the room. It should not be an afterthought. Itemise all the objects to be stored and then plan accordingly. Often one big unit is very effective, as it can house the television, sound equipment and other paraphernalia you have. Don't feel restricted to the wall units most commonly available. You can experiment with materials and styles yourself if you have the necessary

Examples of colour used with conviction to create dramatic and exciting results.

The basic framework of this room is in neutral and tranquil colours, the interest being introduced through the upholstery fabrics. The chair upholstered in a terracotta fabric provides a strong contrast, unifying and strengthening the rest of the room.

equipment or, alternatively, there are plenty of very attractive options, like a jonkmanskas or a big handsome mahogany cupboard that can be fitted out to house whatever you need it to. It can be an elegant addition to the room as well as providing necessary height. If you cannot afford the real thing, there are many exciting ways of transforming a plain cupboard using an interesting style or detail. You can limewash or bleach the wood, paint it or even do some interesting stencilwork.

Books are very often stored in the living room and the subtle tone of a bookcase full of books can be very attractive. Books add substance to a room. Ensure that the shelves are strong enough to carry the weight of the books and that they don't sag in the middle. Other objects can also be stored successfully along with the books – the odd artwork dotted around the shelves can provide an interesting contrast to the books. Baskets can provide an attractive alternative, especially for things like children's toys. Storage shouldn't be thought of only in terms of hiding things away. It also involves display, so things should be arranged carefully. If you have a collection of objects that you would like to display think about how you will do it from the start if it is to be a feature of the room.

Lights

Lighting plays a very important role in the living room. So many different activities take place there that all require specific lighting. It has to be as versatile as possible. Lighting gives a room its atmosphere. Certain lights can create special effects, making a room seem bigger or cosier, minimising structural problems or highlighting certain objects.

Bear in mind the requirements of your life style and the effects that you would like to achieve with lighting in the planning stages of your room. As changing the position of lights and lamps usually involves rewiring , it is obviously better to do it all before the final coat of paint is applied.

When choosing light fixtures, don't think of lighting only it

The eclectic mix of patterns, fabrics and textures creates a strong personal statement.

terms of the lamps and light fittings but also in terms of the quality and kind of light that a specific fitting will produce. The fittings that you choose should suit the style of your room. If your home is an old one and the existing light fittings need replacing, it is possible and often preferable to buy old ones from an antique or junk shop.

Lighting can be categorised by its function. There are three main groupings:

1. Overall, General Lighting

This includes all sources of light that illuminate a large area. It includes the conventional pendant and ceiling lights, spot and downlights and fluorescent lights. The problem with the conventional pendant or ceiling light is that it tends to flatten shadows and does not provide sufficient light to work or read by comfortably. It also tends to lend a dull quality to a room. Spotlights can provide very satisfactory general lighting, although they can also be used for other effects. Fluorescent lighting gives off either cold, white light or a slightly warmer effect, depending on

A distinct and convincing mood of another era is created by the choice of colours, furnishings and the objects displayed.

the colour of the tube. Its greatest disadvantage is that the light it gives off is generally harsh and very bright and it minimises surface interest and shadows and drains colour.

2. Directional Light

This involves a concentrated light aimed at a specific area that serves either to highlight an object or feature or to provide enough light to work by. Spotlights and downlights can be used very effectively for this purpose. A wide range of spotlights is available and they can be mounted in a variety of ways – onto a ceiling, a wall or a track amongst others. The track arrangement can be very useful, as it makes it possible to supply various separate fittings from one electrical source without having to go to the expense of extra electrical work. It can also be recessed into a ceiling. Spots aren't the only possibility: you can also mount down or floodlights or a mixture of the three on a track. It is the various bulbs that produce the different effects. An ordinary

bulb will give off a soft, all-over light. A floodlight will produce a wider, less intense cove-shaped light and a spotlight will provide a concentrated circle of light.

Details made the difference. Here, appropriate light switches are used to carry through the style of the rest of the house.

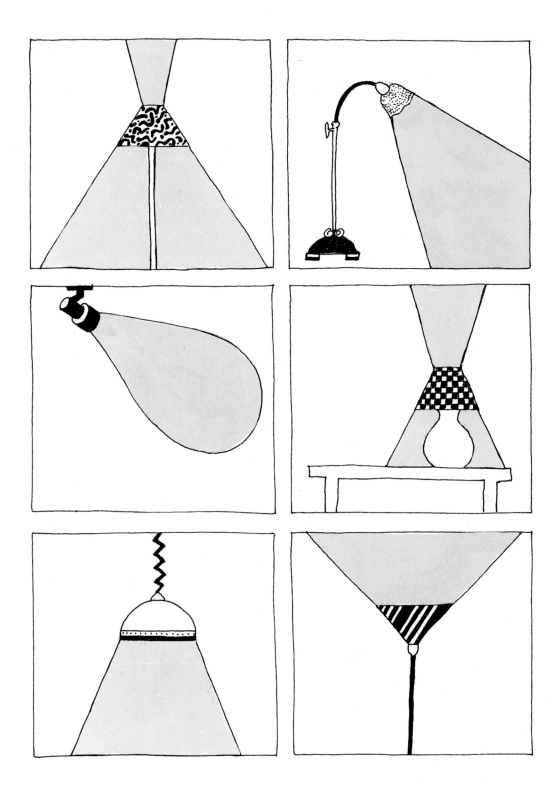

3. Atmospheric Lighting

Uplights, which are spots that, as the name suggests, face upwards, are possibly the most effective at creating atmosphere. They can be positioned behind large pieces of furniture or plants to give a dramatic emphasis, adding interest and mood that is impossible to achieve by day. If you create a mixture of up and downlights, spots and reading lights, you should create an intimate and relaxing atmosphere.

Cascades of inexpensive fabric create an opulant tone for the room.

In trying to create atmosphere in a room the shadows are as important as the light. Lighting should be subtle. This can be achieved with table and floor lamps and wall lights. Pendant lights can be put to good effects with a dimmer. In any lighting scheme that involves spots or floodlights, dimmers are essential. Not only do they save energy, they also allow you to manipulate the mood created by the intensity. If you place lamps on low surfaces with the light coming from underneath the resulting opaque shade will create an intimate atmosphere.

Some ideas

An evenly lit room can lack interest. Try to balance light and shade. The effect will be more dramatic.

It you wash a wall with a downlight the space will seem larger. Downlights can also be used combined with spotlights to enhance the textures of a room if they are correctly positioned. (To wash a wall a downlight is positioned against the wall with the edge of the light just touching the wall.) Conversely, if you want to minimise the texture of a wall, aim the spotlight at the wall.

Uplights set into the corners of a room will attract attention

The variety of pieces of fabric used, provide the unity and interest.

to the edges of the room. It they are placed behind big plants they will throw interesting shadows on the walls and ceiling.

Once you have sorted out the basics of your rooms, it is time to accessorise them. This would be the final stage in the decorating of the rooms.

By accessories, we mean curtainings, wall adornment, decorative detail, collections and many other little things found in a living room. Although many of these accessories may well become a permanent part of your living room, they need not do so. They can be seen as short-term arrangements, as they are simple to change and therefore you need not restrict your choice to the best quality durable products – although, of course, it is imperative that you like them very much all the same. Accessories can be used to introduce colour, pattern texture and excitement into the room. It is very often through them that your personality and sense of humour are revealed.

If you choose carefully and wisely this need not immediately be a very expensive operation. If you have been wise and have spent the major part of your money on the basics you will most likely be on a particularly tight budget at this stage. This could well be an advantage, as you should really do this part slowly over quite a period of time.

If you cannot afford the curtaining that you would really like immediately, start off with an inexpensive neutral fabric like bleached hessian, calico or k-sheeting that blends in with the rest of the room. Likewise, pictures need not be expensive works of art. You can frame virtually anything and you don't have to restrict youself to what is traditionally seen in a frame. Apart from postcards and writing paper, pieces of fabric, a beautifully embroidered table mat, unusual decorative objects can all be framed and displayed on your walls. Alternatively you can hang unframed objects on the wall, such as a fobwatch, masks or plates. With a bit of imagination you can do the framing yourself

Personal style is revealed by what you choose to hang on the walls — all the more so when you include your own artworks, as done here. These pictures are attractively displayed in a well considered arrangement.

— here old frames from second-hand shops can be put to use most successfully.

Like every other stage in the decoration of a room, this one also needs to be carefully considered. Don't display anything that you are not completely happy with. Pictures and ornaments must be hung as a well thought-out composition. Small pictures randomly scattered over the walls have very little impact; it is better to use them in a tight arrangement. Displays, whether of pictures or objects, provide an alternative focal point and their positioning must be planned well. It is ideal to have an attractive view or focal point from all seating positions, so that your living room looks interesting no matter where you are sitting. As pictures will generally be looked at by people who are seated, hang them at a seated eye level.

The living room is an ideal place to display a collection, whether on shelves, in a display cabinet or on a table surface. Although you should avoid too many collections or ones that are too big, they can be both interesting and exciting features of your room. Ornaments must be selected, organised and displayed in a planned and confident way. Curtaining serves both a functional and a decorative purpose. It provides privacy and keeps out the sun, light, cold air and noise. It also serves as a frame around your view of the outside world. There is an enormously wide range of styles and effects of window treatment. Make sure that the type of curtain treatment you choose works well with the decoration of the rest of your room. If you are lucky enough to have a beautiful view from your living room window choose a window treatment that is simple and doesn't distract attention from the view.

The treatment of the curtains can affect the visual proportion of your room. The curtains should fall either to floor length or to sill length if you are to avoid tampering with the proportion of the window frame. If the ceiling is low and you would like to give the impression that it is not, you can

A neutral shell provides the framework for an interesting collection of colours, fabrics, patterns and textures.

Austrian blinds, one of many possible blind treatments.

hang curtains and blinds from the ceiling.
Consider carefully the colours, pattern and drape of the fabric your have chosen. A small window in a small room will appear unbalanced if you use a large print and hang curtains to sill length. Likewise, a very large expanse of window will look a little ridiculous with a small granny print. It is not always necessary to make conventional curtains with the fabric you choose; you can drape the material over a rod most effectively or make it up into a wide variety of blinds. If you are planning to use a heavyweight fabric like velvet or a heavily embroidered Jacquard, the curtains must at least reach the floor to achieve the best drape.
It is important for a room to have a mix of colour, pattern and texture if it is to have visual interest and substance.

The warm wood tones of the jonkmanskas complement the stripped oregon pine doors. Inexpensive ticking has been used most successfully to upholster the couch.

Simple shutters in the right setting can be a perfect solution to window treatment.

Contrast in these areas is vital to emphasise the beautiful things about a room. This does not mean that the contrast needs to be very strong; a very subtle contrast can be just as effective.

The decorative role of flowers is very often underestimated. The effect that a magnificent bowl of flowers can achieve will generally far exceed their cost. A colourful arrangement of flowers can give even the plainest of rooms a feeling of freshness and quality difficult to achieve in any other way.

The living room should be adaptable to the demands of your style and should never be seen as a static and permanent arrangement. It is a room that should grow and develop with you and your family.

Even though the dining area has been integrated into the main living space, it creates a formal character of its own. The room as a whole as well as the furnishings of the dining area complement those of the lounge area.

Eating Rooms

These days eating does not take place only in the dining room. Many people take their meals in the kitchen, while others take theirs in an area that forms part of the general living space. Almost any space can be adapted to be used as an eating area. Regardless of where you eat your meals, if it is to be a place where good food and good conversation are happily savoured, certain basic aspects need to be considered well when planning the decoration of the space.

The table is obviously the focal point and the centre of any eating area. However, although it is always very nice to have a beautiful table, you can cover up a host of sins with a tablecloth and an interesting setting. As long as the table is

stable and the right size you can make do with an uninteresting one until you can afford the table of your dreams. Dressing the table is an area where you can let your creativity loose to achieve impressive results with a very ordinary table and at no great cost.

Chairs need to be given a fair share of consideration — they need to be comfortable so that you can relax and enjoy a nice long meal. Although you can play around with draping and upholstery, if the chairs are unattractive, it is difficult to hide them. There is no need to buy a fully coordinated dining room suite. A collection of different chairs, which you love, linked by some common aspect can often be just as effective and even more interesting. You

A family-orientated eating area that forms part of a kitchen. The decoration is treated in a simple but very colourful way.

can link them by upholstering them all in the same colour of fabric. In this way you can buy pieces that you really like, one at a time, and build up your set slowly.

It is best to avoid having a cluttered table and eating space and therefore storage, especially a cupboard that doubles as a sideboard, is a great boon. A sideboard or a serving space is very useful in keeping the table from getting over-crowded.

The lighting should ideally be both atmospheric and practical. Very often the use of the space is not restricted to meals alone and the lighting needs of the other tasks to be done need to be thought of when the lighting is planned at the start. A dimmer switch is perfect for a multipurpose space, so that at the turn of the knob a well-lit work space can be transformed into a cosy intimate one.

The kitchen and eating space need to be linked to prevent the food from getting cold in transit and to facilitate the transport of the dishes and eating paraphernalia to and fro. If you have young children try to ensure that the surfaces are washable and that the area is reasonably childproof if you are to relax and enjoy your meal. As meals are very often the only time one relaxes together as a couple or a family in one place without the distraction of the television, a relaxed and comfortable environment is vital.

What's Cooking

You can get a tremendous amount of satisfaction out of planning, designing and creating your own kitchen. The kitchen is above all a practical room and if you plan it well, bearing in mind all your needs and requirements, the resulting kitchen will add greatly to the ease and quality of your life. In most homes the kitchen is the most important room, the heart and soul of the home, often doubling as a living and dining room or laundry. A great many hours are spent there, a great many things are stored there, so it makes sense to devote very special attention to every aspect of the room.

A well-positioned window makes maximum use of a beautiful view and a very pleasant spot to work in.

Kitchen renovation can be very deceptive. What may appear to be minor and uncomplicated change may prove prohibitively expensive if, for example, services such as plumbing, electricity or gas are involved. On the other hand it is possible to transform your kitchen relatively inexpensively with colour and a bit of woodwork. Whatever it is that you plan to do, make a budget and find out how much things are likely to cost before you embark on the project and find you have to stop halfway. Bear in mind the degree of expert help you will need. Don't try anything like electrical wiring or plumbing yourself, unless you are qualified in that area. Add 10% to the total of your budget for incidentals. Rather renovate in manageable sections if you cannot afford to do everything you plan to immediately. In any event, it is usually preferable not to rush into a new, complete kitchen. It is such an important room in your home that it really should grow with you. As every family is unique and has different tasks, needs and budgets each will tend to emphasise specific qualities and aspects. However, regardless of these differences there are a few fundamental requirements for any successful kitchen.

Working Surfaces

These should be as plentiful as possible because they will be used not only for food preparation but also probably to house appliances such as kettles and toasters. The main

food preparation areas should ideally be between the stove and the sink. The ideal length is just less than two arms length. A central island or wooden kitchen table can also provide useful work space if you have sufficient room in your kitchen for one. At the same time it makes the room more inviting and provides space for family meals and shared pots of tea.

Sinks and Stoves

The two main activities in the kitchen, food preparation and washing up, should dictate to a large extent the layout of your kitchen. The sink, stove and fridge should form a work triangle. No two of these should be more than a double armspan apart; neither should they be too close. The stove must be within easy reach of the sink, so that pots and pans can be easily carried backwards and forwards. Avoid putting your stove or sink in a corner or your stove under a window. Curtains, if used, should be a good distance from the stove. A sink works well under a window − near a good souce of ventilation and light.

Storage

Bearing in mind how many things are stored in a kitchen, storage is obviously of prime importance. Not only do you

Right: Three different storage units are combined attractively in this corner. The glass cupboard doors show off the interesting collection of jars.

Below: Very practical storage features like this roll-down hideaway for appliances and the spice drawer increase the accessibility of regularly used objects to streamline kitchen work and reduce kitchen clutter.

An extremely efficient, very well-considered kitchen. There is plenty of work surface, especially where it is most needed — around the hob and the sink.

need plenty of it, you also need many different kinds of storage. Utensils, crockery and cutlery in daily use need to be more accessible than less frequently used objects. Some food will obviously need cold storage, other well-ventilated racks and other still well positioned shelved dry cupboards. Owing to the structural constraints of kitchens, some cupboards will be more accessible than others. To ensure that your kitchen is functional and efficient, it is vital to plan storage space with a great deal of thought.
Aspects to be considered are:
● Depth — the deeper things are stored in a cupboard, the more inaccessible they become.
● Width — extra appliances may need to fit on top of the cupboard.

● Proximity to other areas — crockery and cutlery must be near the sink, foods must be near the stove, etc.

Make a list of all the things that need to be stored in your kitchen and work out how many cupboards will be needed to store them. Bearing in mind all these considerations, work out a ground plan for the room. Working to scale on graph paper, make cutouts of the cupboards and appliances you have, as well as those you plan to get (washing machine, stove, fridge, dishwasher, etc.). Shuffle the cutouts around until you have a satisfactory arrangement. The smaller your kitchen, the greater will be your challenge to make maximum use of space. Well utilized

Left: Space under the sink is cleverly used to store cleaning materials and dishwashing liquid.

Below: Another example of specific storage fulfilling a specific purpose. Here equipment needed for cooking is as close at hand as possible.

and cleverly planned space with specific storage features can be very pleasing aesthetically.

Electricity Plugs and Points

Before you finalise your cupboard positions, make sure that the electricity plugs and points are exactly where they need to be. Bear in mind the expense of moving them and all the appliances that will need electrical outlets – the fridge, kettle, toaster, mixer, iron, etc.

Lighting and Ventilation

Both lighting and ventilation are essential to create a kitchen that is a relaxing and an efficient work space. You should have at least one big window and if possible an outside door. Try to ensure plenty of natural light in the kitchen. It is ideal to have a window facing north.

Artificial light is just as important. Try to avoid using a central fluorescent light. It tends to make everything look very flat and colourless. You will probably need both bright, direct light and dimmer, indirect light, especially if the kitchen is to be used for eating and entertaining. Spotlights work very well in the kitchen, where they can illuminate specific work areas. Alternatively, small strips mounted on

the base of top cupboards will light up specific work spaces without being obtrusive.

Kitchen Style

The materials and style that you choose for your kitchen fittings will dictate the overall feel and look of the room. There are three types of kitchen cupboards: fitted units, shelving and free-standing furniture. They can be used exclusively in a high-tech, clean-line fitted kitchen or combined in a family, country-style kitchen. All three types have their advantages and disadvantages and all three have endless possiblilities, depending of course on your needs, tastes and budget.

Fitted Units

Although fitted cupboards are perhaps not as major an undertaking as plumbing or electrical work, if you do not have the necessary tools and expertise, it would be advisable to approach an expert to make them for you.

It is best to have a very clear idea of what you want to have done before you approach anyone if you want to avoid ending up with cupboards that fall short of your needs. Try to see some of the kitchens already made by your chosen company or carpenter to make sure that the finish and quality are as you would want them to be. There are numerous kitchen companies. Try to choose one with a good reputation.

If you have a particularly small or oddly shaped room, it may be worth your while to think about a custom-built kitchen.

The most successful work surface on fitted units is post-formed Formica, which prevents the problem of dirt col-

lecting in joints and cracks. These come in many colours and many finishes. The granite effect can look very impressive and the wood finish works well with wooden furniture or floors. It is very useful to have a marble or solid wood work board built into the work surface. Make sure that all the edges are properly sealed.

Shelving

Shelving is a much less expensive alternative to fitted cupboards and with the right tools you should be able to tackle their construction yourself. There are plenty of possibilities here, ranging from a pigeonhole system to shelves of varied heights and it remains for you to decide what you want and need. Shelving is particularly effective if you have beautiful crockery or interesting kitchen utensils to display. Open shelves are obviously best suited to tidy people.

Free-standing Furniture

Free-standing furniture suits a more informal and homely approach. This normally involves more clutter and demands a fairly large space. A small kitchen will generally need the discipline of fitted units. Free-standing units have the advantage of being transportable, so that you can happily invest in pieces of furniture that you will keep and use in more than one home. They increase the flexibility of

Top: Light streams in through extended windows brightening up what was originally a dark room.

Above: The playful use of colour makes this a very cheerful kitchen table setting.

your room, as you can easily change the furniture if you grow tired of it or if it is no longer suitable.

A style of furniture in fairly good supply today is traditional cottage furniture. The clinical look of many modern kitchens often tends to isolate the kitchen for the cook only and the atmosphere is neither relaxing nor inviting. By in-

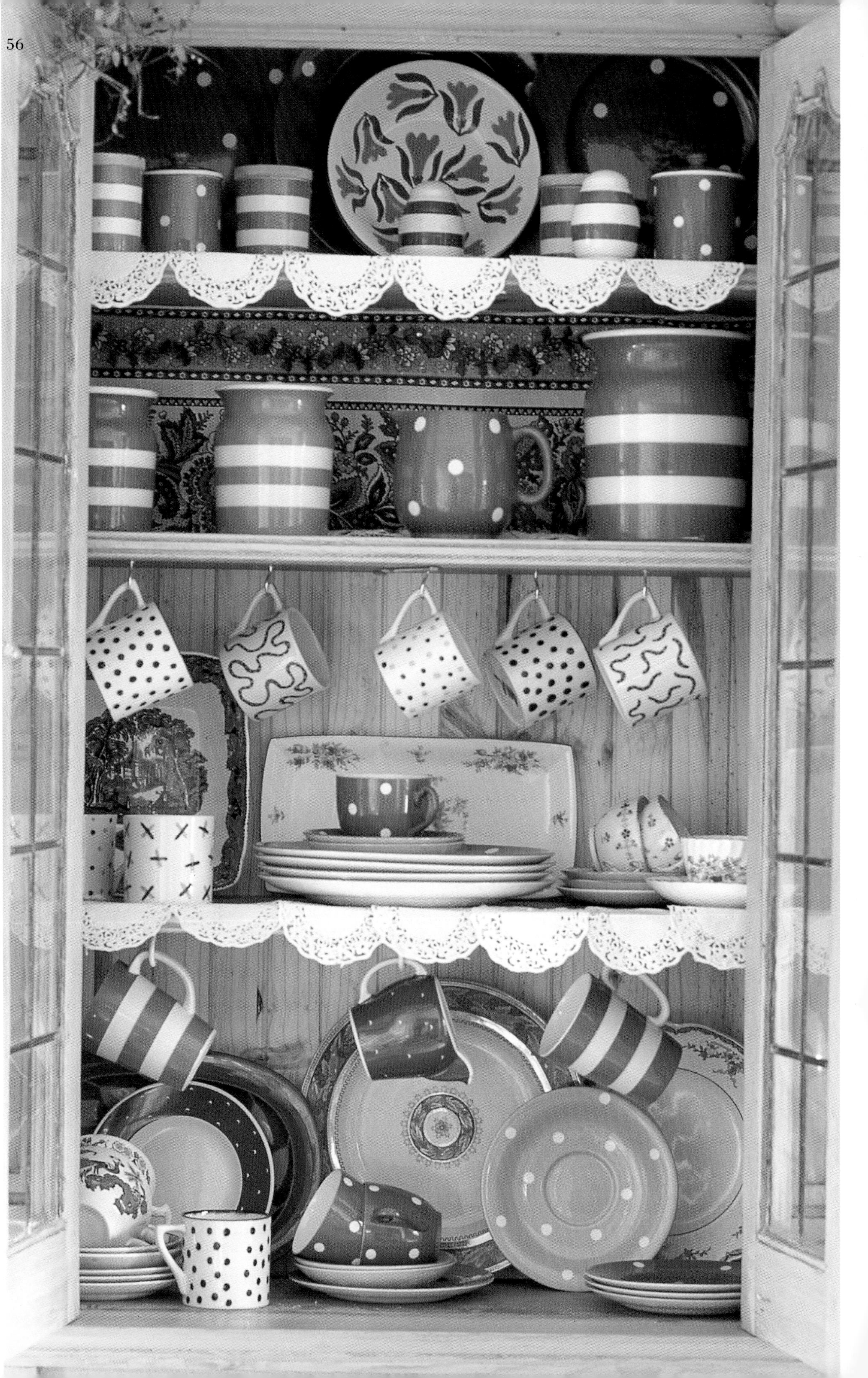

A freestanding dresser, while a very practical storage unit, is also an attractive feature of this kitchen.

The colouring of the cupboard is complemented by the objects stored in it to create a visually appealing feature.

Joyful use of colour combined with the natural wood creates a cheerful display.

troducing well-worn wood and relaxing and comfortable furniture, the kitchen immediately becomes a warmer, friendlier place. The disadvantage of free-standing furniture is that it is not nearly as space-efficient as fitted units and it is not as easy to keep clean.

Dressers can function well for both storage and display. Separate shelving units can be suspended from a wall or can rest on top of surfaces. Oregon pine furniture is the most freely available and, if you are patient, you can find reasonably priced, interesting pieces, enabling you eventually to put together a stunning kitchen that costs less than a fitted one. A further bonus is that fitted units eventually show wear and tear, whereas old wooden pieces normally age gracefully and usually increase in value with age.

Often when moving into an old house you are faced with outdated and tatty fitted cupboards. Before you automatically rip them out, think about fixing them up and working with them. Perhaps you could replace the surfaces and give the cupboards a coat of paint. Otherwise, you could possibly strip the paint off the wooden doors. Another option is to remove the doors of the top cupboards and have them replaced by glass and wooden doors. This style of cupboard should blend very well with free-standing units. If you are a bit dubious about how hygienic old rustic furniture is and you would prefer something less rickety, excellent copies of old styles are now being made.

Free-standing units are imaginatively combined with old-world objects to achieve a nostalgic appeal. Attention to detail and some bright contrasts result in truly convincing, cosy décor.

The great advantage of putting together this kind of kitchen is that it can be done over a lengthy period of time. Neither need you compromise on the style and quality of the completed kitchen; you can make do with what you have until you can afford the next piece.

A kitchen full of free-standing furniture and shelving units is much more visual, with the emphasis on display and colour. Bottled food and fried flowers add life and interest to the room. Baskets combine well with wood and are very handy to store vegetables, cutlery and dishcloths. Remember that displayed kitchenware needs to be washed regularly, as it will quickly get dusty and grimy and the attractive effect will be lost.

There are many other areas where you can introduce your personality and style into your kitchen. When you choose a style that you really like make certain that you follow it through in all the details. If you lower your standard and include things in your kitchen that contradict the rest of your style, the room as a whole will lack honesty.

Colour is probably the most obvious way of introducing interest to a room. Here we do not mean that you must choose one tone of a specific colour and that you should buy all your utensils and dishcloths in that colour. If you decide on one colour, explore it, collects objects in many shades and tones of that colour. Blue is a very popular colour for the country-style kitchen and an abundance of lovely old crockery, beautiful teapots, kitchen utensils in florals, stripes, spots and rich solid colour is available. A completely white, more modern kitchen can look fresh, clean and very impressive. A combination of colours can also be very exciting. Do not ignore the wonderful colours of food and the value of displaying it – the natural tones of dried food, the crisp, bright colours of fresh fruit and vegetables, the interesting textured tones of bottled honeycomb or preserved apricots add interest and freshness to your kitchen.

Walls and Floors

Many of the materials used on the kitchen walls can also be used on the floors. Both surfaces need to be easy to clean

Magnificent oak fitted units work well with terracotta tiles. The kitchen table surrounded by an interesting collection of chairs looks inviting as well as providing an extra surface. Lights are concealed under the top cupboards, providing direct light for working without detracting from the cosy atmosphere.

and need to be water and steam-resistant. Paint walls with washable acrylic paint and if you do use wallpaper use a fungicidal adhesive to prevent mould growth.

When choosing the floor treatment try to ensure that it works well with the style of the rest of the kitchen. To a certain extent your choice will be limited by the subfloor you have. For example, a quarry tile floor will be too heavy for a secondfloor room. If you plan to put down a new floor, consult an expert before you start. Prevent making any expensive mistakes. A kitchen floor needs to be smooth and flat, so that dirt does not collect in nooks and crannies. Often it is best to pay a professional, especially if you are laying marble. Ceramic, marble and quarry tiles can all look very impressive and normally they wear very well. However, they have the disadvantage of being cold to walk on. If you live in a subtropical region, like Durban, this will probably suit you very well. In colder areas, it is possible to install underfloor heating, quite inexpensively, while you lay the floor. Linoleum is probably the most common and inexpensive of kitchen floor treatments available. It has the advantage of being easy to clean and being quiet to

walk on. There is a wide selection of linoleum to choose from in many colours, styles and textures. If you are lucky enough to have a wooden floor, it is well worth stripping and sealing it. Warm wood lends a comfortable, homely atmosphere to a kitchen, although it does need to be resealed regularly.

How often one hears that it is the quality and finish of the kitchen and bathroom that is the selling point of a home. Whatever your ultimate intention for you home may be, it is clear that money well spent in the kitchen should definitely exceed the value of the investment. Perhaps more important is the ultimate test of any kitchen: whether it is a room that people enjoy being in and most of all whether it serves its purpose well.

Under the covers

The bedroom is a very personal and private space that should ideally be a peaceful retreat from the mad chaos of life. Unless the room is to be used for other purposes as well, the whole emphasis of the decoration of the room should be on comfort and relaxation. Most people have quite strong views on what their ideal bedroom should look like and yet in reality it is very often the last room to be decorated.

The tranquil, cool colour of the walls is an interesting backdrop to the dark wooden furniture.

The dressing table, being a personal space, is the perfect area to treat as you please.

should not be overlooked. There is a wide selection of beds and bed treatments, ranging from the simple to the very ornate and you need to think very carefully about the style you choose, as it will set the tone for the rest of the room. As the central focus of the room, the bed can be either dressed up or dressed down, depending on how you intend decorating the rest of the room. Bed linen comes in a tremendous variety of patterns, colours and shapes nowadays, enabling you to change the look of your bedroom from an Arabian palace to a country cottage just by changing the bed linen. However, if the look is to be convincing it must be carried through to the decoration of the rest of the room. Even in traditional, plain white linen there is a large choice in terms of quality embroidery detail, pillowcase style and frills. It is often the simplest bed treatment that is the most effective.

It is just as well to plan the complete decoration of the bedroom from the start, even if you are able to afford only a bed. It is advisable to have a well thought-out master plan

If you are limited in terms of either money or space you are presented with the challange of a definite framework around which to work. Think of it in terms of having to be ingenious rather than of having to skimp. Although you will probably pine for all kinds of terribly expensive things for your bedroom that you can't afford or can't fit in, never allow yourself to forget that it it style, clever choices and thorough consideration that makes for an attractively decorated bedroom and not money alone.

The area to spend most of the bedroom budget on is the bed and especially the mattress. It is, after all, the most important piece of furniture in the room. Money saved on the mattress will not be worth it, even if the rest of the room is stunning. Nonetheless the decorative aspect of the bed

for the future so that every change in the room is a step in the right direction.

The next on your list of priorities should be storage. The smaller the room, the more careful your planning will have to be. The ideal is to have a separate dressing room or walk-in closet. This will not only reduce the clutter and make it easier to keep the room tidy, it will also give you more space, including more wall space, to work with. Sadly, generally most people don't have the extra room for a dressing room and have to accommodate storage in their bedrooms. Fitted cupboards have the advantage of providing maximum storage space by using the full height of the room. Although increasing the value of the home, their disadvantage is that they become a permanent fixture that can become dated and they cannot be taken with you, whereas a free-standing handsome old cupboard is transportable

Dark panelling gives an old-world feeling to the room. It is brought to life by the contrast of the light duvet cover and the white mosquito net.

and very often turns out to be a good investment. In the end, it is all a matter of personal taste and convenience. The cupboard should echo the character of the room. All the woodwork in the room should preferably be painted to match. If you have lovely wooden pieces of furniture this obviously doesn't apply, although it can be attractive to strip the window and door frames and picture rails to their natural wood. If your bedroom is very small and you need the cupboards to blend in with the walls to increase the effect of visual space, the cupboards can be given the same treatment (wallpaper, paint, stencilling, etc.) as the rest of the room. Extra care, however, is needed to achieve a professional finish if you use wallpaper.

If the bedroom is to be really comfortable and relaxing, the colours that you choose to decorate it in are very important. Colour can completely alter the feeling of a room. The colour of a room affects people's moods and the way that they feel about the space and must therefore be considered carefully. To illustrate this fact there is a true story

about a factory where the staff were constantly complaining of the cold and where the heating bills were exorbitant. The management, in desperation, repainted the blue walls yellow and the results were immediate and remarkable. Right away the staff felt happier, there were no more complaints about the cold and the heating bills dropped.

Warm colours and especially soft colours like subtle pinks, oranges and yellows are the most comforting colours and pick up even the faintest winter sunlight. Cooler colours like soft blues and greens, although tranquil, are best suited to a warmer climate. Although it can create an unusual and dramatic room, a colour scheme that is very vivid and bright will often prove to be more disturbing than relaxing. Another disadvantage is that you will probably tire of it more quickly than more subtle colouring. If you would like to use bright colurs rather use them in areas that are easy to change, like the bed linen, pictures and accessories. Contrast within each element of texture, pattern and colour is fundamental to a satisfactory end product. By this, we

Here an old cupboard has been revamped to provide storage that suits specific needs.

A classic traditional bedroom where the bed was the original source of inspiration.

mean that if you are to appreciate a texture, for example, you can only do so by using it in combination with a different texture.

The whole range of wall treatments can be used most effectively in the bedroom from paint, wallpaper, stencils and borders to murals. The bedroom is a good place to try out different paint or stencilling techniques. If you use a border it can be positioned just under or above the picture rail or at windowsill level. It often works well to paint the area below or above the border in a different colour.

The bedroom ceiling is perhaps the only one in the home that is looked at as much as any other part of the room. It therefore offers wonderful possibilities to be made a feature of. You could do this in many different ways - contrasting paintwork, stencilling, exciting light fittings or even a

fresco are but a few possiblilities.

If you have a very small bedroom, it is often best to treat it in the same light colour. White is particularly suitable, as it will make the room seem bigger. A mixture of busy patterns will make the room feel cluttered and smaller, so if you use a pattern stick to one design and preferably choose a print with a light background. Keep in mind that space can be as much a matter of feeling as of actual room measurements. A feeling of spaciousness can be achieved very easily with the clever use of lighting, mirrors, pattern and the furnishings you choose.

Make full use of mirrors. A huge old mirror, used as a headboard will give the impression that the room is twice its actual size, especially if the mirror reflects a window. It will also have the added advantage of introducing more

The richness of the wood is emphasised by the warm yellow of the walls. The contrast makes the furniture stand out as graphic elements in the room.

light into the room. These effects can also be achieved by covering an empty wall with mirrors or positioning a mirror at a right angle to a window.

When it comes to flooring, carpeting is the ideal choice, as you will often be walking barefoot. As the bedroom carpet seldom suffers from the wear and tear of other rooms, you needn't buy the best quality or a sensible colour. Stripped wooden floors can seem rich and beautiful but are best covered with a rug of some kind. Tiles or a patterned carpet in a diagonal or geometric design will make the room seem larger.

Lighting is as important in the bedroom as elsewhere. The fixtures themselves are very often features of the room and at least should complement the style of the room. The main lighting needs are for reading, make-up application and providing a relaxing and possibly romantic atmosphere. A pair of bedside lamps is important in order for one partner to read while the other sleeps. These can be either placed on bedside tables, attached to the wall behind the bed or set into the ceiling. Make-up lighting needs to provide light that is thrown into your face. The ideal is a downlight positioned directly above the dressing table. If you are planning to use the room for other purposes like sewing, working or watching television, obviously your lighting needs will increase and you will have to make provision for them. Lighting can also be used to give the impression of increased space. An uplight or two in the corners of the room will make it seem larger at night.

Curtaining takes up a lot of visual space in the bedroom and should also be carefully considered. If you are plan-

Interesting and effective use of colour combinations create a comfortable and appealing setting.

An exceptional collection of old perfume bottles displayed in a bedroom.

Uncluttered furnishings and simple colours make this room a relaxing and peaceful place.

ning to match the curtains with the wall colour, it is better to have a contrast than an inexact match that doesn't work. The way you treat your window can be adapted to the mood of the room, whether it be romantic, dramatic or minimalistic. If you are lucky enough to have a beautiful, unusual window, show it off rather than covering it up. This is often best done by treating the window as simply as possible.

The most important role of curtaining in the bedroom is to keep out the light and cold and to provide privacy. So, whichever treatment you choose - whether blinds or curtains - make sure that it will ensure you as much privacy and block out as much light and cold as you personally require.

If the bedroom is to take on the role of other rooms as well, careful consideration will need to be paid to the decorative element. Furniture in the bedroom should be decorative as well as functional to avoid the room looking cluttered. The decorative qualities of furnishings are as important as the practical ones. Beautiful furniture is worth waiting for and spending money on, as it is a real pleasure to live with and it gives your home its character and uniqueness.

Water works

Certainly, an exciting bathroom is a challenge. There are certain limitations that dictate exactly what you can do with a bathroom. More than any other room in the house its decoration and fittings are dictated by the uses to which it is put. It is therefore obvious that functional planning takes precedence in the design of your bathroom. This does not mean that your creativity should be restricted. To the contrary, it should pose an exciting challenge, a definite framework around which to work.

A very simple and rustic bathroom making good use of an old cast-iron bath and a wooden washstand.

Planning

Typically, you are faced with a small room and very specific fittings. The treatment of the walls and floors needs to be carefully considered and must be water and steam-resistant. The room may also have to double as a laundry with a build-in washing machine and dryer. Besides the practical uses of the room, one shouldn't neglect the therapeutic and pleasureable aspects. The bath is often a wonderful warm haven of peace where you can relax and un-wind after a hectic day. It's a room to pamper yourself in and a comfortable wicker chair can be a cosy addition.

Before your start planning to move the bath or other fittings around bear the cost in mind. Plumbing is a major expense in the bathroom and, as far as possible, it is generally financially wiser to leave fittings where they are.

Before doing anything ask yourself the following three questions:

● What do I want out of my bathroom, what look am I hoping to achieve - do I want something exotic and luxurious or something utilitarian and splashproof?

● What can I afford to spend?

● How much room do I have to work with?

Your answers to these will go a long way in determining a framework for you to work with. Bear in mind that the bathroom, like the kitchen, is an important selling point in your home. Decorate it as well as you possibly can. Spend your money wisely. Try to avoid bright, fashion colours in your fittings and tiles. Not only will you tire of these colours sooner than plain, light colours but you will also create a fixed colour scheme that you cannot alter without considerable expense. Certainly use bright colours if you wish but rather introduce them in the wall colour, the shower curtain, the blinds and other accessories. Remember too that sloppy tiling can detract from even the most beautiful of tiles and fittings, so if you can't guarantee your workmanship it will be well worth your while to pay a recom-

Above: The black and white tiling repeated on the border of the wall is a clever but simple way of introducing interest into the bathroom.

Top right and right: This children's bathroom lends itself to a fun, lighthearted approach. The handmade ladybirds were a family project.

mended expert to carry out such work for you. The plumbing must work well - nothing can be more frustrating than a toilet that won't flush or slow-running water. Here too, hire an expert. It will be worth it.

The Basics

Your choice of fittings will depend entirely on what you can afford, what is appropriate to the style of your house and whether it is viable to keep the existing fittings. If your bathroom works well as far as plumbing and space usage go but the fixtures are looking the worse for wear, consider renovating them before automatically throwing them out.

This basin is dropped into the black marble slab of an old washstand. The authentic character is carried through to the brass taps.

Baths, basins and even toilets can be renovated or re-enamelled by a professional firm. There are many companies in most Yellow Pages that will do this for you. The taps can be rechromed, power-coated or rebrassed beautifully. The outside of an old bath can be painted, stencilled or panelled to make it an interesting feature. Another option is to extend the surround of the bath to create a shelf with room for books and plants.

Baths

In South Africa the three most common baths are the traditional cast-iron one, the pressed-steel bath with various enamel finishes and the cheaper acrylic bath. Obviously the first two are stronger and will last longer that the plastic ones. An extra-long bath can be very comfortable, especially for tall people, but has the disadvantage of using more water. Low, sunken baths can be tiresome to clean and are not ideal for bathing small children but they can be used to good effect in rooms with low ceilings.

Showers

Showers are generally more space-efficient and more economical than baths. However, unless they are well considered, they are generally not as attractive as baths. If you are going to combine the bath and shower choose a flat-bottomed bath with a nonslip surface. Protect the

The use of wooden panelling in the bathroom is both decorative and functional.

bathroom by adding a plastic-lined curtain or preferably, especially in a family bathroom, a fitted glass or plastic door.

Walls

Walls must be steam and water-resistant, particularly if it is a small room where there is little ventilation and high steam build-up. In any event, the walls next to baths and basins must be water-resistant. If wallpaper is used in the bathroom, it should be placed only above several rows of tiles or alternatively it should be covered in either perspex or glass around the splash-prone areas or painted with a clear eggshell glaze. It is best to avoid using wallpaper in small bathrooms and particularly in well-used family bathrooms, as it will soon start peeling off the wall.

Panelling can work very well as an alternative to tiling. It suits old Victorian fixtures and can be used to good effect in hiding unattractive piping. If you use standard tongue-and-groove boards, which come in a variety of thicknesses, combined with mouldings, which are available at any timber merchant, you can create a very attractive finish. It can prove more reasonable than tiling and you do not need to replace the tiles hidden behind the panels. If you are renovating an old bathroom using the original fixtures it

can create a very authentic look.

Although tiling is expensive, it is the most effective surface in a bathroom and should not need any attention for many years. Your tiles needn't be patterned or exotic. In fact, it is often better to use plain cream or white tiles. You can add interest by using a border or by changing the colour of the walls or wallpaper. Inexpensive white tiles can look very impressive if laid imaginatively, combined with a few more special tiles or surrounded by an exciting border. Fabric can work as well as the paper borders commercially available. Like paper borders it is applied with wallpaper glue.

Floors

The floor covering doesn't need to be predictable or overly ostentations either to be effective. It does, however, require careful consideration. It must be both water-resistant and easy to clean. Carpets can make a bathroom seem luxurious and cosy, especially in a cold climate, but they are best avoided if the floor is to be regularly splashed by over-energetic bathers. In all events, don't fit wall-to-wall carpeting; rather leave it unfitted, so that it can be taken out to dry. If you are lucky enough to have a wooden floor in your bathroom, an attractive rug or kelim can be a stunning feature. Tiles or Novilon would obviously be your best choice

The old oregon pine door in this small bathroom has been cut in half so that is can fold back on itself in order to save space.

for splashers. Here too, interesting detail in pattern and colour can be introduced by the way in which the tiles are laid. Marley tiles, a local option, are available in an enormous range of colours. They are very pliable and are fairly easy to cut into designs and can give very exciting and unique results.

Other alternatives are quarry tiles, which are ideal in a rustic bathroom and combine very well with wood, or mosaics, which if used imaginatively can add to a fresh, Mediterranean style.

Lighting

Good, direct lighting is important for shaving and applying make-up. Ideally, softer, indirect lighting should be used to provide the atmosphere for that peaceful and relaxing bath.

Windows

An elegant or unusual big window can be a glorious feature in a bathroom, especially on a bright and sunny morning. A few luxurious plants planted directly behind it would make it even more so. An ugly window or a very small one can be hidden attractively with blinds or curtaining. Obviously you will need some sort of screening at the

window. On a small window, etched opaque glass or stained glass can be beautiful but this will not necessarily work on a large window. A soft, filtered effect can be achieved by using louvres, glass shelves filled with plants or wooden shutters. If you are planning to keep plants in your bathroom make sure that they are plants that thrive in a warm, damp environment.

Storage

Storage is an aspect not to be overlooked in the bathroom. It is well worth your while to draw up a list of everything you need to store in the bathroom – towels, medicines, toiletries, laundry basket, nappy bucket and so on. Most people store medicines in the bathroom and for this you really need a childproof catch. A very handy place to store toiletries and towels is in a vanity unit under the basin. This need not be a cupboard – an attractive curtain surrounding it can be as effective. Hooks are very useful in the bathroom and can be used for everything from face cloths to bags of bath toys. Towel rails, of course, are necessary – a heated rail is a wonderfully luxurious option, not only for warming towels but also for drying them quickly.

As a bathroom is usually a small room, it is necessary to pay close attention to detail and finish. The small details

A grand old window has been installed here to add a new dimension to this elegant bathroom.

can make a big difference. Nowhere is compromise more visible than in the bathroom. The curtains or blinds, the towels, the bathroom mat and all the normal bathroom clutter must be considered. A pile of thick white towels in an immaculate but plain bathroom can introduce a feeling of style and luxury. Mirrors can make a big difference to a bathroom. A wall of mirrors can double the visual space of a small bathroom. A framed mirror can play a decorative as well as practical role if it works well with the rest of the room.

A bathroom can be a good place to show off an interesting collection – a display of old bottles, perfect seashells placed on narrow glass shelves across a wooden window frame, a few beautiful plates mounted on the wall or even a couple of attractive pictures can add charm and interest to the room.

Possibly the easiest way to achieve a dramatic effect in the bathroom is through the use of colour. Colour can be introduced not only on the walls but also in the towels, bathroom mats and all the bathroom detail. Black and white is a wonderful classic bathroom colour scheme and works particularly well in older houses. If the bathroom is

very small it is best to keep the room in a single, light colour carried through to the towels and curtaining.

It is easier to create a relaxing, enjoyable atmosphere in a bigger room. It will be more conducive to using the room for other purposes such as those of a dressing room or home gym. If you have a view and privacy, position the bath near the window so that you can enjoy the view. If the bath dominates the room, surround it with a low platform to give it a sunken effect. Alternatively, if you have the space introduce a comfortable piece of furniture.

Toilets

As with all bathroom accessories a vast range of colours and a smaller range of styles are available. What is becoming increasingly popular are wall-hung toilets. These toilets have the advnatage of being more hygienic and facilitate the laying of floor tiles, providing a neater finish.

Besides the range of acrylic toilet seats available it is now possible to purchase traditional wooden seats hygienically treated in a durable gloss finish. Although these look at home in an old-style bathroom they are equally effective in a modern, high-tech environment.

Often the simplest decoration can be very impressive.

A wide variety of wall treatments can be used in a bathroom. Here is a particularly appealing combination.

With toilets even more so than with any other bathroom fittings, buy the best you can afford, as compromise can cost you a great deal more in the long run.

Basins

Within the range of colours and styles that is offered, three fundamental types are available. The wall-mounted basin is reinforced internally and requires no further support, although brackets for support are available. These are mounted directly onto the wall.

The drop-in basin is also available in a large range of colours and styles. It can be recessed into almost any kind of surface. In this country, a large variety of beautiful washstands is available: a basin could be dropped into the marble surface or a new marble slab could be used to replace a damaged and cracked surface. Perhaps you have stone or wood, which can easily be cut to size and your basin dropped into such a surface. These obviously require proper sealing; your hardware store can advise you on this – especially on the surface that you intend sealing and that is required to be splashproof.

Formica is also suitable and comes in a huge range of colours and finishes. The granite surface is particularly effective. Remember the practical limitations of your space when selecting a basin. It should not only be practical and comfortable; it should also suit the design of the bathroom.

If you decide to remodel a washstand or chest of drawers to take a drop-in basin, make sure the unit you have designed is at a comfortable height for washing your hands and clothes, as this will be problematic if it is either too high or too low.

The third choice is the pedestal basin. The pedestal can be an interesting feature and has the advantage of concealing plumbing.

There are more possibilities for imaginative and exciting bathrooms than you may at first suppose. You will need to look at everything that is available and explore different ways of using them in your room.

Conclusion

Our main concern in this book has been to impress upon you that personal style isn't something out there in an expensive interior decorating shop that you can buy but, rather that it is an essence within yourself. Many people never discover or develop this outward manifestation of their personality and this is in itself a great pity.

One of life's great pleasures is surely to create for yourself a unique and honest home environment that is not only aesthetically pleasing and is moulded comfortably around your life style but that is above all, a true reflection of your style and your taste. The decoration of your home should reflect how you live and who you are. Just as your life is never static or unaffected by changes and circumstances, neither should your home be. If your home is always to be exciting and interesting, it should constantly be in tune with your life style and personal growth. By this, we do not mean that there should be no constant items amongst your possessions. On the contrary, much of your home should be permanent. It is really the details and the arrangement of the furniture that can provide the new interest.

A confident approach is vital if you are to create convincing and successful results. The effect will be lost completely if it appears in any way to be fragmented or tentative. You can decorate your home in any way you choose as long as you carry your plan through and it is very clearly thought out. Although spontaneity is very important, you should consider very carefully every change or addition to your home.

Some areas such as window treatment and paint techniques have only been touched on. There are many excellent books on these subjects and so we leave these areas to the experts. This book is intended to be a guide to be used in conjuction with your own imagination and ideas.